VERONICA B. W

P9-DNK-416

A *Simple Way* To
Read
Through
Your Bible
Your Plan, Your Pace, No Stress!

Unless otherwise indicated, all scripture references are taken from the Authorized King James Version.

Scripture quotations marked (AMP) are taken from the Amplified® Bible. Copyright ©1954, 1958, 1962, 1964, 1965, 1987 by the Lockman Foundation. Used by permission. (www.Lockman.org)

Scripture quotations marked (NKJV) are taken from the New King James Version®. Copyright ©1982 by Thomas Nelson, Inc. Used by permission. All rights reserved.

Scripture quotation marked (NIV) are from the Holy Bible, New International Version. Copyright© 1973, 1978, 1984 International Bible Society. Used by permission.

A Simple Way To Read Through Your Bible
ISBN 10: 1-59544-531-5
ISBN 13: 978-1-59544-557-5

Copyright 2014
Bill Winston Ministries
P.O. Box 947
Oak Park, IL 60303-0947

Printed in the United States of America. All rights reserved under International Copyright Law. Contents and/ or cover may not be reproduced in whole or in part in any form without the express written consent of the author or Bill Winston Ministries.

Table of Contents

Dedication

This book is dedicated to the countless members of
God's family who
have had to force themselves
to read the Bible because
their parents made them,
their pastor commanded them,
they kept falling asleep,
or their conscience condemned them for
neglecting it.

In lieu of a super hero to
"save the day,"
let's just make a
proper introduction, and
take the relationship slow.

Don't get intimate too quickly.
Get to know one another,
you and your Bible.

Let the butterflies flutter in your stomach.
Give the goose bumps a chance to emerge.
Don't try to unveil these truths too quickly.

Intimacy with God begins slowly.
He won't expose His deepest truths
on the first date.

He'll save something for next time.
He'll reveal just enough so you'll look forward
to seeing Him again.

He's not looking for a one night stand.
He's in this relationship for eternity.

Introduction

Have you ever made a personal commitment to read through the Bible in one year, only to find yourself on December 31 to be only three-quarters of the way completed? The sincerest plans (especially the spiritual ones) too many times get placed on the back burner as we try to fulfill the urgent matters that arise on a daily basis.

Well if this sounds like you, there is a way to fulfill your promise to yourself every time you read through the scriptures. Just keep track of the chapters you read by crossing off each chapter on the chart included in this book. On days you want to saturate yourself in the Word, read to your heart's content, and note accordingly.

When life gets hectic, just continue from where you last left off. You read at your own pace, with no pressure to adhere to a specific time deadline.

The last year I tried to read through the Bible, I didn't finish until March 15 of the following year! But because I had created my recording chart, no sweat! The next reading time I just started back at Genesis, and using this "round robin" format, I became free, once and for all, from the pressure to fit into the 365-days-a-year box.

We invite you, if you have not done so already, to begin reading through the Bible, continually, until Jesus comes for His Church. (The recording chart can be found in the back of the book.) Reading beyond our favorite passages to get a more holistic view of scriptural events is enriching and eye opening. You will learn so much about God, Jesus and the Holy Spirit, God's true nature, His covenant relationship with Israel and the Church, His plan for mankind, about yourself and your immense potential!

We have also included brief summaries of every book of the Bible, from Genesis to Revelation. These are simply to "introduce" you to each Bible book. Just as meeting someone new includes only a brief statement of introduction (and not their life history), the description of each Bible book is just enough to put it in perspective, so you can understand what you're reading.

We encourage you to access reading material that goes into further detail, if you find your "spiritual appetite" needs more substantial sustenance. This book serves you, the reader the "appetizer" from a lay person's perspective, not a biblical scholar or university professor. Consider this text a primer, to get you started on your Bible journey with training wheels, until you can cruise on your own, finding your own resources and following your own "rabbit trails" down the path of biblical truth.

Foreword

When my wife was using her faith to believe God for a husband, she expressed two requirements to God. She desired a man who loved God with all his heart, and one who studied the Word of God more than she did!

Aside from this desperate request disclosing her desire to get married (just kidding!), it reflects the love and priority she gives to God's Word. She insisted that whoever she was to spend the rest of her life with must share that same regard for God and His eternal Word.

And true to form, our courtship was a bit unusual, as compared with most other relationships. Most of our time spent together or on the phone was filled with discussions about the Bible and Christian books we had read.

So as her "unconventional" dedication reflects, she truly does see her relationship with God and His Word as an eternal relationship.

After more than thirty-one years of marriage, we both are still "going strong" in our pursuit of secrets and mysteries hidden in the pages of our well-worn Bibles. Yes, we do have electronic versions, but every time we open up the treasures of those leather bound writings, we are reminded of the hours and hours spent with God while studying the scriptures. Every highlighted word, every dog-eared page, every tape-repaired tear, is evidence that we have said "yes!" to God's invitation for a life-long relationship.

I whole heartedly invite you to partake of the fruit of her relationship with God, by using this book to inspire you to read through and really get to know your Bible. I have dedicated my life to study, teaching and preaching the gospel to reach all nations with the truth; to set the captives free and reposition them to the place of leadership God has ordained for them from the foundation of the world. The Bible is the one living resource that mankind needs to recoup his dignity and once again become the blessing that his Creator has ordained for him to be.

Keep walking by faith!
William "Bill" Winston

Prayer to Reveal the Word

Thank you Father, that when the Word of the Kingdom
is sown and grown in me
it becomes the greatest of all the plants in my heart
Reveal to me your wisdom laid up for me
and for those who I teach
Cause wisdom to enter my heart
and knowledge to be pleasant unto my soul
Unveil to me your truth and cause me to be wise
and to inherit glory
Enlighten the eyes of my understanding
Teach me secrets and mysteries of your Kingdom
Reveal your majesty and power
Impart to me your compassion and your heart
Comfort me and fill me with faith
Lead me in the way I should go
because the light is in the Word
A lamp unto my feet and a light unto my path
Deliver me from all temptation
and cause me to walk in your statutes
Feed me with the Bread of Life
Equip me with the sword of the Spirit
Cause me to partake of the divine nature
through your precious promises
Make me a doer of the Word and not a hearer only
Make your truth my shield and buckler
Wash me and prune me through your Word
I receive your Word to dwell in me richly
To be life to me and health to all my flesh
Uphold me and my family with the Word of your power
Transform me by the renewing of my mind
Give me more understanding than all my teachers
Disciple me as I continue in your Word
I receive your truth to make and keep me free
Quicken me according to your Word

Holy Spirit, guide me into all truth
Show me things to come
Reveal to me things freely given to me of God
Help me to frame worlds with the Word of God
I speak the Word only; whatsoever I do shall prosper
And the Father within me does the works
I study so I am prepared for every good work
Teach me Lord, as I meditate your Word day and night
Root up every plant in me you have not planted
And sow the Word in me
that I may bear much fruit that remains
To multiply, replenish the earth and subdue it with the Blessing
May your Word through my mouth
release and create your will in the earth
in Jesus' Name, Amen!

GENESIS

Outline of Genesis

Summary of Genesis

The book of Genesis introduces the reader to the beginning of all things: the creation of the universe and all planets, earth, all living plants and creatures, mankind, marriage, family, and nations. Genesis also tells us of the origin of sin in mankind through the tempter satan, and the destruction of all life (except Noah's family and selected animals) through a flood, because of the wickedness of men.

God establishes a covenant with Abram (later renamed Abraham), and his descendants. Obedience to God will bring blessings back to earth. Abraham became the beginning of a family and a nation that will give birth to the Messiah, who will pay the ultimate sacrifice for man's sin, thus opening the way for mankind to be perfectly restored to God and enjoy eternal life.

Abraham's son Isaac was born to parents too old to have children but by faith he was conceived and born. Isaac's son Jacob, a trickster, through life experiences is transformed into the patriarch Israel, having twelve sons. Joseph, his eleventh son, though hated by his brothers, eventually rises to become second in command in Egypt, saving that nation and his family from famine.

EXODUS

Outline of Exodus

Ch 1	Children of Israel in Slavery
Ch 2—4	Moses' Birth & Calling
Ch 5—11	Challenge to Pharaoh & Plagues
Ch 12—13	Passover
Ch 14—19	Exodus & Initial Problems
Ch 20—24	Giving of the Law
Ch 25—40	Building of the Tabernacle and Offerings

Summary of Exodus

In the opening chapters of Exodus, Jacob's (Israel's) twelve sons have become (over 400 years) more than two million people enslaved to the Egyptian pharaoh. God calls Moses, a Hebrew raised by pharaoh's daughter, to confront pharaoh and demand of him to "let My people go." After a series of miraculous plagues and the parting of the Red Sea, Israel travels to the wilderness.

Having been enslaved for generations, the faith and blessings of their Abrahamic heritage have faded. God promises to bring them into a land flowing with "milk and honey," but their identity is no longer God's chosen people but patterned after Egypt, riddled with fear, immorality and idolatry. Possessing God's best would require fighting giants, and the majority of the nation simply did not believe God was able to give them victory. So, they wandered in the wilderness forty years, and their children got to enter the Promised Land.

God gives Moses "The Law" (Ten Commandments). He also gives him moral, social and religious laws for conduct and worship; establishes the priesthood; and instructs them to build a portable tabernacle so God may dwell among them, His presence being known by a pillar of cloud by day and a pillar of fire by night.

LEVITICUS

Outline of Leviticus

Summary of Leviticus

God gave Moses laws for Israel (the nation Israel, the descendants of the man Israel) to follow in their worship and service to God and for everyday living. Everything and everyone had to be holy, cleansed, sanctified or consecrated before God.

From the food they ate, the way they treated one another, and the cleansing of their bodies to the service of the priests and the sacrifices brought to God—there was a specific manner in which everything was to be done to come into God's presence and to maintain fellowship with Him. Feasts to keep and sacrifices to offer for sins.

Behind every sacrifice and tradition was a type and shadow of Jesus Christ, their redeemer, later to be revealed to the world.

Thank God for the Holy Spirit who now sanctifies us with the truth!

NUMBERS

Outline of Numbers

Ch 1—4	Organizing Israel
Ch 5—10	Sanctifying Israel
Ch 11—25	Complaints, Problems & Judgment: The Wilderness Generation
Ch 26—27	Organizing the New Generation
Ch 28—30	Sanctifying The New Generation: Offerings, Feasts and Vows
Ch 31—32	The Battles Begin
Ch 33	Detail of Cities in Wilderness Journeys
Ch 34 — 36	Instructions on Distributing the Land

Summary of Numbers

In the opening scene of Numbers, thirteen months after the flight from Egypt and the parting of the Red Sea, we see Israel taking a census of all men over the age of twenty years able to go to war.

The camps of the twelve tribes (families) of Israel are stationed around the tabernacle (a large tent where religious practices occurred) in the sign of a cross. Work assignments were given to the Levites, and instructions on sanctifying Israel were given.

Murmuring and unbelief surfaced time and again, so that this first generation was sentenced to die in the wilderness. After forty years, the new generation is sanctified, wins their first battles, divides the spoil and begins to possess the land God promised to Abraham and his seed.

DEUTERONOMY

Outline of Deuteronomy

Ch 1—4	History of the Wilderness Generation
Ch 5—26	Codes of Conduct for the Joshua Generation
Ch 27—33	Consequences of Conduct: Blessings and Curses
Ch 34	The Death of Moses

Summary of Deuteronomy

Deuteronomy takes place at the end of Israel's forty year wilderness journey, and the end of Moses' life and ministry. He calls the entire nation of Israel together and teaches them in three segments.

First, Moses shares with the new generation their nation's history with God over the past forty years.

Next, he teaches them God's commandments, statutes and judgments, beginning with the Ten Commandments. These are laws by which Israel was to obey and serve God so that they may be victorious in battle as they possess the land and be blessed above all people as they obey God. It teaches them to live by God's high standards of conduct as a nation. Moses reiterates the laws already given regarding sacrifices, tithing, worship and daily life.

Lastly, Moses spotlights the good blessings that will follow their obedience, and warns them of the tragedies that will befall them if they refuse to obey. God knew they would not be able to keep all His laws perfectly, so He instructed Moses to implement a practice of animal sacrifice to atone for, or cover their sins.

It is in Deuteronomy that God promises that His people could enjoy "the days of heaven" upon the earth.

JOSHUA

Outline of Joshua

Ch 1—5	Natural & Spiritual Preparation to Take the Land
Ch 6—12	Conquering the Land
Ch 13—22	Dividing the Land
Ch 23—24	Joshua's Final Words

Summary of Joshua

After Moses' death, Joshua is assigned by God to lead the nation of Israel into possessing the "land of promise" that God initially promised to Abraham, then to Isaac and Jacob. Through a series of battles, they learn that guaranteed victory comes from obedience to God's commands, not solely by military might.

After many years and battles, the land and the spoils are divided up among several of the tribes. In Joshua's final words, he admonishes Israel to continue to possess the land not yet taken, and to continue to keep God's laws.

JUDGES

Outline of Judges

Ch 1	Tribes of Israel Fail to Drive Out Enemies
Ch 2	Israel Follows Idolatry
Ch 3—16	Fourteen Judges of Israel
Ch 17—21	A Close-up Look at Israel's Sins

Summary of Judges

After the death of Joshua, the tribes of Israel failed to drive out their enemies from the land they sought to possess.   Their disobedience to God's laws removed God's help to win battles, and they adopted the idolatrous ways of the nations they should have dispossessed.

The next generation forsook God altogether, and began a repetitive cycle of successive generations going from bondage to their enemies, to deliverance through the leadership of judges that God would raise up.

The book of Judges ends with the tribes of Israel fighting against one another, and everyone doing that which is right in his own eyes.

RUTH

Outline of Ruth

Ch 1	Tragedy Brings Naomi (& Ruth) Home
Ch 2	Ruth Finds Favor with Boaz
Ch 3	Ruth Pursues Boaz
Ch 4	Ruth & Boaz and the Lineage of a King

Summary of Ruth

The story of Ruth takes place during the period of Judges. In a time of famine, Elimelech and his wife Naomi travel from the land of Israel to the country of Moab with their two sons.

Elimelech dies, his sons grow to adulthood, marry, and they too die. Ruth, one of Naomi's daughters-in-law, vows to go back with Naomi to Naomi's home country, serve her God, and dwell among her people.

Upon their return, Ruth gains favor with a relative named Boaz, while gleaning in his cornfields (as the poor were allowed to do.) Through Naomi's wise advice, Ruth wins Boaz's heart, and becomes his wife.

I SAMUEL

Outline of I Samuel

Ch 1—3	Transfer of Leadership: **Eli to Samuel**
Ch 4—7	Transporting of the Ark
Ch 8—10	Transfer of Leadership: **Samuel to Saul**
Ch 11—13	Reign, Philistine Battles
Ch 14—17	Transfer of Leadership: **Saul to David**
Ch 18—26	Saul's Pursuit of David
Ch 27, 29, 30	David & His Army
Ch 28, 31	Saul & His Destruction

Summary of I Samuel

In I Samuel we witness the rule of the last two judges of Israel, the priest Eli and the prophet Samuel. The elders of Israel desire an earthly king like the nations surrounding them, so Samuel reluctantly anoints Saul to be king, and admonishes both the nation and the king to fear and obey God.

Saul fails to keep God's commandments, and God sends Samuel to anoint another, David, a shepherd, to be king. David's heroic acts in battle cause such anger and jealousy in Saul that Saul tries repeatedly to kill David, who escapes capture by the protective hand of God. The close of I Samuel shows Saul's sons slain by the Philistines in battle, and Saul taking his life by his own sword.

II SAMUEL

Outline of II Samuel

Ch 1—4	David's Reign Over Judah From Hebron
Ch 5 — 10	David's Reign Over Israel And Victories in Battle
Ch 11—12	David's Sin and Judgment
Ch 13—18	David's Family Troubles
Ch 19—24	David's Kingdom Troubles

Summary of II Samuel

In the opening chapters of II Samuel we see David mourning the deaths of Jonathan and Saul, and an ongoing war between the house of Saul and the house of David. David rules as king over Judah for seven and a half years, then over all of Israel for another thirty-three years.

David's devotion and close relationship with God was the basis of his success as king, as military strategist, and as worship leader. He was truly a man after God's own heart. He prayed before battles and got God's plan of attack, which guaranteed victory time and again. His armies fought and won many battles, and took a great store of spoils.

David's successes come to an end when grave sin enters into his life, and judgment falls. The problems in his own family start a snowball effect of tragedies, which ultimately affect the welfare of the entire nation of Israel, culminating in a plague that claims the lives of many thousands in Israel. The plague is stopped when David offers burnt offerings and peace offerings upon the altar he built at the threshing floor of Araunah, the Jebusite.

I KINGS

Outline of I Kings

Summary of I Kings

King David is now very old, Solomon's half brother Adonijah makes a failed attempt to steal the throne, but Solomon is quickly anointed king. On David's deathbed, he charges his son Solomon to walk in God's ways, and to execute judgment against those who betrayed David. The Lord appears to Solomon in a dream, and grants Solomon wisdom, riches and honor above all the kings of the earth. Solomon builds a massive temple (designed and funded by David) to replace the tented tabernacle. He brings the Ark of the Covenant from Zion, and has a ceremonious, anointed dedication service.

Solomon's unbridled love for many women of the heathen nations drew his heart away from God, and his kingdom was taken from him and given to his servant (an officer in Solomon's army). The nation was split into two kingdoms, and one tribe, Judah, remained with the house of David. (Actually, I Kings 12:21,23 tells us that the tribe of Benjamin also joined Judah under King David. The tribe of Levi stayed under David too.) Many kings rise and fall in each kingdom, including the infamous King Ahab, ruler of the Northern Kingdom. Elijah arises as God's prophet to boldly speak the Word of the Lord to Ahab, which God confirms with signs and miracles following. Ahab finally does repent, and judgment against him is delayed until the next generation.

II KINGS

Outline of II Kings

Ch 1–2	Transition from **Elijah to Elisha**
Ch 3–9	Elisha Ministers to Kings and Individuals
Ch 8–16	The Rise and Fall of Kings of Israel and Judah
Ch 17	**Israel's Final Defeat;** Carried Away to Assyria
Ch 18–24	The Reign of Many Kings of Judah
Ch 25	**Judah Conquered,** Taken Captive to Babylon by the Chaldees under Nebuchadnezzar

Summary of II Kings

The prophet Elijah ends his ministry with a grand departure on a chariot and horses of fire, caught up into heaven in a whirlwind. Prophet Elisha now follows his footsteps, meeting the needs of various people seeking help from God—showing us that even in the midst of a rebellious nation, God will still hear and miraculously answer those who seek the Lord.

More wicked kings rise and fall in both the Northern and Southern Kingdoms of Israel, until their rejection of God causes God to reject them. Even though some of Judah's kings served God, it wasn't enough to turn the nation back to Jehovah.

The Northern Kingdom of Israel is besieged by Assyria, dismantled, and taken away captive. Years later, Judah, the Southern Kingdom, is invaded by the army of the Chaldees, and taken away captive to Babylon, under the leadership of King Nebuchadnezzar.

I CHRONICLES

Outline of I Chronicles

Ch 1—9	Genealogies (From Adam to those who returned to Jerusalem after the Babylonian Exile)
Ch 10	Summary of Saul's Reign
Ch 11—12	Establishing the Kingdom of Israel (Through David's Military Forces)
Ch 13—17	David Brings the Ark of the Covenant to Jerusalem
Ch 18—20	David's Military Battles
Ch 21—27	David's Preparation and Provision for Building the Temple

Summary of I Chronicles

First and Second Chronicles were originally a single book. It is believed that they were written many decades after the Jews had returned to Jerusalem, following their seventy year exile in Babylon, to teach the new generation (and the remnant still living) their history and to encourage them as they rebuilt their nation.

This book provides a detailed record of genealogies and King David's accomplishments. First and Second Chronicles focus only on the history of Judah, from a priestly vantage point. Great emphasis is placed on the spiritual heritage of David, the Ark of the Covenant, preparation for building the temple, priesthood duties, work assignments, and some of David's key military victories.

The time period and some events of I Chronicles are approximately the same as in II Samuel. It's the same story from different perspectives, each book focusing on different details. First Chronicles covers more of the temple preparation & building; II Samuel covers more of David's personal and military triumphs and tragedies.

II CHRONICLES

Outline of II Chronicles

Ch 1—7	Solomon's Reign and Building of the Temple
Ch 8 — 9	The Glory of Solomon's Kingdom
Ch 10—36:16	The Reigns of Twenty Kings of Judah
Ch 36:17—21	Judah Captive in Babylon Seventy Years
Ch 36:22—23	King Cyrus Releases Jews to Return to Jerusalem

Summary of II Chronicles

The book of II Chronicles covers the time period from Solomon's reign to the release of the Jews from Babylonian captivity.

In the opening chapter we see God granting Solomon wisdom, riches, wealth, and honor. Solomon begins, completes, and dedicates the magnificent Temple, the House of God, during a glory-filled worship service. Thousands of animal sacrifices were offered. King Solomon surpassed all the kings of the earth in riches and wisdom.

The following three-fourths of the book describes the rule of the next twenty kings of Judah, the Southern Kingdom. It ends with a brief account of Judah's captivity in Babylon and their release (after seventy years) by King Cyrus.

A few kings from the Northern Kingdom are mentioned only in passing, and were not a main focus of this book. Many of the events and time periods covered in II Chronicles are the same as in I and II Kings.

EZRA

Outline of Ezra

Ch 1—2	Return to Jerusalem Under Zerubbabel
Ch 3—6	Rebuilding the Temple
Ch 7—8	Return to Jerusalem Under Ezra
Ch 9—10	Sanctification of the People

Summary of Ezra

Seventy years have passed since the first group of Jews was deported from the land of Judah to Babylon. Cyrus, king of Persia, has overthrown Babylon and the Chaldees the previous year, and allows the first group of almost 50,000 captives to return to Jerusalem, under the leadership of Zerubbabel.

The Lord moves upon Cyrus to generously finance the reconstruction of the Temple, which had been destroyed. Adversaries rise up against the Jews and delay the building program. Haggai's and Zechariah's prophecies to Judah bring them strength and faith to finish building.

Nearly sixty years later, Ezra leads a second remnant from Babylon to Jerusalem, to re-establish the traditional worship, Temple instruments and sacrifices for the Temple. The book of Ezra ends with Ezra's prayer to God and Israel's repentance for marrying wives of the idolatrous nations and not sanctifying themselves unto God.

NEHEMIAH

Outline of Nehemiah

Ch 1—7   Rebuilding the Wall
Ch 8—13   Restoring the People

Summary of Nehemiah

Nehemiah, a cup bearer in the Persian king's palace, became burdened upon hearing of the reproach of the Jews who had returned to Jerusalem after the seventy-year captivity. The city was devastated, the walls broken down, and the people were in great affliction.

Nehemiah obtained favor from the king, and much provision, to go to Jerusalem and rebuild the walls and gates. Though many enemies sought to hinder them, they continued to build and completed the wall in fifty-two days.

A historical record was made of all the families returning to Judah. Ezra read the law to them, and they fasted and repented of their sins. The Priests and Levites re-established their covenant with God. They cast lots to decide which ten percent of the population would reside in Jerusalem. Finally, some cleansing of the house of God took place and setting in order observances of the Law.

ESTHER

Outline of Esther

Ch 1–2	Esther Becomes Queen
Ch 3–5	Haman's Wicked Plot
Ch 6–7	Haman's Plot Foiled
Ch 8–10	Jews Triumph over their Enemies

Summary of Esther

The book of Esther shows how powerfully God can use an ordinary person to fulfill His purposes. Esther and other Jews were still in the land of captivity. She was favored and chosen in a national beauty contest to replace Queen Vashti as wife to King Ahasuerus.

Haman, one of the king's top officials, hated Esther's cousin Mordecai (and all Jews) because he would not bow down to Haman. Haman got the king to agree to wipe out all Jews, but through Esther's entreaty the Jews were allowed to fight and defend themselves. Haman ended up hung on the gallows he intended for Mordecai, and Mordecai gets promoted in the kingdom. An annual national holiday is established for the Jewish people in remembrance of the day they were spared extinction.

JOB

Outline of Job

Ch 1—2	Disasters of Job
	Discussions: God and Satan
Ch 3—37	Discussions: Job & Friends
Ch 38—42	Discussions: Job & God
Ch 42	Deliverance of Job

Summary of Job

Job is thought to be one of the earliest books of the Bible, set in the time of the Patriarchs. In the opening scene is a discussion between God and satan, then shows Job losing his family, his wealth and his health. He laments with his friends trying to find out "why me?" Finally, after an encounter with Almighty God, everything is restored to Job, twice as much as he had in the beginning.

PSALMS

Outline of Psalms by Division

Ch 1—41	Associated with Genesis-41 books
Ch 42—72	Associated with Exodus-31 books
Ch 73—89	Associated with Leviticus-17 books
Ch 90—106	Associated with Numbers-17books
Ch 107—150	Associated with Deuteronomy-44 books

Topics Covered in the Book of Psalms

Psalms Prophesying of the Coming Messiah
Psalms of Thanksgiving
Psalms of Praise and Worship
Psalms of the Greatness of God's Attributes and
    What He Can Do
Psalms of God's Creation, Heavens and Earth
Psalms Declaring the Good Things God Has Done
Prayers for Help
Prayers for Deliverance from Enemies
Psalms Describing People Who Are Against God
Psalms of Vengeance Towards Enemies
Psalms Declaring the Punishment of the Wicked
Psalms of the History of Israel
Psalms of Fellowship with God
Psalms of the Author Seeking God
Psalms of Repentance to God
Psalms of Wisdom
Psalms Affirming Faith and Trust in God
Psalms of the Author Pouring Out His Heart to
    God Because of What He's Experiencing
Psalms About the Word of God

Summary of Psalms

The book of Psalms is a collection of Hebrew songs and

poetry, written and compiled over a one thousand year time period, from the time of Moses through Ezra. Compilers have divided Psalms into five major groups. Each group is associated with one of the first five books of the Bible, because the content of some of the Psalms in that section have the same theme as those first five books.

In the book of Psalms, we get an intimate look into the heart of the writers, their joys and pains, and their victories and defeats. We see how they see God, and what they say when they pray, seek, worship and fellowship with God. We see a wide range of emotions from awe and admiration of God to invoking calamity and bodily hurt to their enemies. (Please be reminded of Matthew 5:44-48, where we're told by Jesus to love our enemies. We have a God that says vengeance is His, so we'll leave that to God.)

Many of these psalms were used in both private and public worship in Israel.

Authors of the Psalms

At least ten or more authors contributed to and compiled (over a period of about 600 years) the 150 chapters of the book of Psalms. Among the authors are David, who wrote almost half the Psalms, followed by, Asaph, Korah, Hezekiah, and others, some of whom remain anonymous. Even Solomon (Ps. 127) and Moses (Ps. 90) were inspired to add their words of poetic verse!

PROVERBS

Outline of Proverbs

Ch 1:1—7	Introduction
Ch 1:8—9:18	Importance of Wisdom and Instruction
Ch 10—29	Proverbs of Solomon
Ch 30	Proverbs of Agur
Ch 31	Proverbs of King Lemuel

Summary of Proverbs

King Solomon, the wisest man of the Old Testament, wrote most of the sayings in Proverbs, to impart words of wisdom to his son. These teachings will lead and safeguard men, women and children as they navigate through life here on earth. The topics cover a wide spectrum of daily life in the home, in the local community, in relationships in business and in government.

Ultimately, the righteous, those who fear and obey God (God's Word), will enjoy God's blessings. The wicked, who refuse to follow instruction will experience calamity. The wise and good man will adopt a lifestyle that brings godly rewards; the foolish and evil man will be rewarded with shame, cruelty, hatred and evil.

The bottom line is that wisdom from God is the principal factor for leading a life pleasing to God and free from the calamities that befall the unrighteous. The "strange woman" has a double meaning: a physical, natural woman who tempts men to lust and to enter into sexual sin; and the "spirit of the world," which lures believers away from the "high life" of righteous living into operating in the "low life" of selfish, fleshly gratification, with no regard for the consequences which are certain to follow. God's wisdom must be hidden in the heart (through study, meditation and memorization) and established as a lifestyle; only then will it speak to us to guide us and deliver us from evil.

ECCLESIASTES

Outline of Ecclesiastes

Ch 1	The Vanity of Life: Looking for Fulfillment in...
Ch 2	Pleasure, Alcohol, Home Estates & Wealth, Music, Self-Indulgence, Accomplishments
Ch 3—4	Vain Philosophy and Human Understanding
Ch 5—6	Riches
Ch 7—11	Dealing with Life's Issues
Ch 12	Final Words of the Aged Solomon

Summary of Ecclesiastes

Solomon, in his later years, is seeing life through the eyes of pessimism and depression. Life has lost meaning because he is disconnected from God. First Kings 11 gives us insight on the reason why:

"Solomon loved many strange women...He had 700 wives, princesses, and 300 concubines:...when Solomon was old, his wives turned away his heart after other gods...and Solomon did evil in the sight of the Lord." He built temples for many false gods. Some say these marriages were for political reasons. God warned him through two personal visitations, but to no avail, so God said He would tear the kingdom of Israel from Solomon and give it to his servant.

The wisdom Solomon was once endowed with is a mere shadow, and his search for meaning in life takes him down dead—end paths. His discovers there is no fulfillment in earthly pursuits as long as man's relationship with God is disrupted. "Vanity of vanities" is his constant cry. Chapter 2:17 sums up Solomon's attitude at this point in time: "I hated life."

This should be motivation enough for believers in Jesus Christ to keep their spirits strong (through Bible study, prayer, attending church services), and to stay faithful in their relationship with God. Let us learn from Solomon's mistakes!

SONG OF SOLOMON

Outline for the Song of Solomon

Ch 1—2   Love Begins: Reflections on Courtship
Ch 3—4   Love and Marriage: Maturing Love
Ch 5—6   Love Words to Spouses
Ch 7—8   Love Grows

Summary of Song of Solomon

The Song of Solomon is written as a poetic play, with the characters being the Shulamite (woman), her Beloved (man), the Daughters of Jerusalem (a chorus) and others. It is a beautiful story expressing passionate desire and love between a man ("my beloved,") and a woman (the Shulamite). The poetry is colorful and full of imagery.

There are at least three distinctly different interpretations of this play.
1. The Shulamite woman's beloved is Solomon and she desires him as he desired her. One writer says this is the only true love that Solomon experienced. The rest of his marriages were arranged for political purposes.
   Act One: Shulamite Woman Longs for Her Beloved
   Act Two: Solomon's Majestic Procession
   Act Three: Courtship
   Act Four: Vows of Love
   Act Five: Final Words

2. King Solomon disguises himself as a shepherd and surprises her when he returns for her in a royal wedding procession. She loves him in return.
   Act One: Shulamite Woman Tending the Vineyard
   Act Two: Solomon Posing As A Shepherd Selects His Bride
   Act Three: Solomon Returns for His Bride and They Are Wed

3. The Shulamite woman actually loves a shepherd (who is not Solomon) and was taken into Solomon's household to become another of his queens. She yearns for her shepherd and refuses Solomon's advances. She finally is rescued by her shepherd lover and they live happily ever after. One scholar says this play reflects God's ideal of one man for one woman, illustrating the love of Christ for His Church.

Whatever the true interpretation is, these verses are excellent material for romance! Let's pray that though hundreds of years have passed since the Song of Solomon was written, that the Holy Spirit will reveal its true meaning and significance for our lives today.

Scholars think Solomon wrote Song of Solomon in his youthful days, Proverbs during his mature years and Ecclesiastes during his older years.

ISAIAH

Outline of Isaiah

Summary of Isaiah

Isaiah was a prophet whose prophecies cover the most expansive range of topics and time periods in the Bible, from the fall of Lucifer from heaven (14:12-17) to the eternal new heavens and new earth (66:22).

Chapter 1:1 says that Isaiah prophesied during the reigns of Kings Uzziah, Jotham, Ahaz and Hezekiah, kings of Judah. Israel had already gone into Idolatry, and Judah was slacking off of God's Word and becoming worldly and carnal in their behavior and lifestyle. Isaiah warned of God's judgment, not only towards Judah but towards other Gentile nations surrounding them, in the first thirty-nine chapters.

The last twenty-seven chapters present a totally different atmosphere, revealing the overwhelming love, forgiveness, generosity and favor of God, and His willingness to restore and bless His covenant people.

The book of Isaiah is quoted many times in the New Testament, and shows the most complete picture of the suffering of Jesus in the Bible, in chapter 53.

JEREMIAH

Outline of Jeremiah

Ch 1	Jeremiah's Calling
Ch 2—33	Prophecies to Judah
Ch 34—38	Prophecies During the Resistance Against Nebuchadnezzar
Ch 39, 52	Jerusalem Falls
Ch 40—42	Remnant in Judah
Ch 43—45	Remnant in Egypt
Ch 46—51	Judgments Against Gentile Nations

Summary of Jeremiah

Jeremiah was called to be a prophet while in his youth. He ministered for more than forty years during the reigns of Josiah, Jehoahaz, Jehoiakim, Jehoiachin, and Zedekiah, Kings of Judah.

A personal side of Jeremiah is revealed, more so than any other Old Testament prophet. We see his heart of compassion for his people as he pleads with them and for them, to repent of their evil ways and return to God. Interspersed among his prophesies (many of which are poetic in form) are dialogs between he and God.

Jeremiah suffered greatly for obeying God's call. His family persecuted him (12:6), his neighbors wanted to kill him (11:21), his peers rejected him, he was arrested, beaten, identified as a traitor and jailed. His prophecies were burned (36:21—23) and he experienced much rejection. He vowed to himself to not speak any more in the Name of the Lord, but he confesses that "His word was in mine heart as a burning fire shut up in my bones, and I was weary with forbearing, and I could not stay" (20:9).

LAMENTATIONS

Outline of Lamentations

Ch 1	Mourning Over the Tragedy of Destruction
Ch 2	The Anger of God and a Call to Prayer
Ch 3	Jeremiah's Suffering and Prayer
Ch 4	The Results of God's Judgment
Ch 5	Prayer for Restoration

Summary of Lamentations

The book of Lamentations was written during the time when Jerusalem was under siege by the Babylonians under Nebuchadnezzar. Judah was in gross sin, and judgment had come. Jerusalem was captured and the city was destroyed.

Jeremiah, in a series of five poems, mourns over Judah and weeps with great sorrow. In the midst of his pain, he affirms, "It is of the Lord's mercies that we are not consumed, because his compassions fail not. They are new every morning: great is thy faithfulness" (3:22–23).

EZEKIEL

Outline of Ezekiel

Ch 1—3, 33	Ezekiel's Vision and Calling
Ch 4—24	Prophecies Against Judah and Jerusalem
Ch 25—32, 35	Prophecies Against Gentile Nations
Ch 34	False Shepherds and the True Shepherd
Ch 36—37	Restoration of Israel
Ch 38—39	Wrath Against Gog and Magog
Ch 40—48	The Glory of God and the Temple

Summary of Ezekiel

Most of Ezekiel's prophecies occur between the second and third deportations of the Jews to Babylon. This priest and prophet use prophecies, stories, signs and dramatizations to communicate God's messages to His exiled people.

He reminds this exiled generation of the cause of their current destruction, the judgment to come upon surrounding nations, and the future restoration of the nation of Israel.

DANIEL

Outline of Daniel

Ch 1	Daniel Excels in Babylon
Ch 2	Nebuchadnezzar's Dream of the Image
Ch 3	Nebuchadnezzar's Image Built
	Three Hebrews Survive the Fire
Ch 4	Nebuchadnezzar's Vision of a Tree
Ch 5	Belshazzar's Vision of Handwriting on Wall
Ch 6	Darius' Decree and Daniel's Deliverance
Ch 7	Daniel's Vision of Four Beasts
Ch 8	Daniel's Vision of Ram and Goat
Ch 9, 11	Daniel's Vision of Seventy Weeks
Ch 10, 12	Daniel's Vision of Israel's Future

Summary of Daniel

Daniel was deported with the first group of Jews to Babylon, and his ministry to the kings in Babylon spanned the entire time of captivity, under Nebuchadnezzar and Belshazzar, then under the Persian kings Darius and Cyrus.

Daniel is an outstanding example of a man of conviction, faith, courage and leadership, who remained faithful in his service to God, even when it endangered his very life. God gifted him to interpret dreams, and he was a great asset and witness to every king he served under.

HOSEA

Outline of Hosea

Ch 1—3   Faithful Hosea—Unfaithful Wife
Ch 4—14   Faithful God—Unfaithful Israel

Summary of Hosea

The prophet Hosea ministers to the Northern Kingdom Israel (called Ephraim), during a time of economic prosperity but spiritual and moral decline. To dramatize the fallen state of Israel, God commands Hosea to marry a harlot (prostitute), Gomer, who continues to be unfaithful to Hosea.

Hosea now understands first hand God's heart of love and patience towards the spiritually adulterous Israel. Though sins of idolatry, evil doing, murder, robbery and rebellion are overwhelming, God still ends with a promise to restore Israel and heal her backslidings.

JOEL

Outline of Joel

Ch 1   Insect Plague and a Call to Prayer
Ch 2   Future Invasion and a Call to Prayer
Ch 3   The Day of the Lord

Summary of Joel

The prophet Joel discloses that the recent insect plague which has ravished the land was a judgment against Judah for their sins. He preaches that the Day of the Lord will bring much greater judgment, but blessings to those who serve Him.

AMOS

Outline of Amos

Ch 1 — 2	Judgment of Nations and Israel
Ch 3—6	Iniquity and Judgment
Ch 7 — 9:10	Five Visions of Judgment
Ch 9:11—15	Promises of Restoration

Summary of Amos

Amos was a shepherd of Judah, called to prophesy to Israel. Israel's religious worship was meaningless. Her oppression of the poor, greed, idolatry, materialism, violence and robbery were the last straw to God. Amos decrees, "Therefore will I cause you to go into captivity..." (5:27) but even then God has a promise to bring them out of captivity to rebuild the waste cities (9:14).

OBADIAH

Outline of Obadiah

Ch 1   Judgment Against Edom

Summary of Obadiah

Obadiah prophesies against the nation of Edom, the descendents of Esau. Edom not only came against Israel, but helped Israel's enemies to defeat her. From the womb, Jacob and Esau (and now their descendents) were at odds with one another. Herod the Great (tried to find and kill Jesus as a child) came from this family line.

JONAH

Outline of Jonah

Ch 1	Jonah Runs but He Can't Hide
Ch 2	Jonah Prays and is Delivered
Ch 3	Jonah Preaches and Nineveh Repents
Ch 4	Jonah Pouts and God Corrects Him

Summary of Jonah

God called Jonah to preach to Nineveh, the capital city of the Gentile nation of Assyria, so they would repent and turn to God. Jonah, not wanting Nineveh to be spared, went the opposite way by ship, headed to Tarshish (twenty five hundred miles west of Nineveh). His disobedience caused a great storm which was calmed when Jonah was tossed overboard. After spending three days in the belly of a large fish (or whale), Jonah gets vomited up on shore and preaches to Nineveh.

The king of Nineveh is so repentant that he even includes the animals in their national fast! Jonah is angry that Nineveh is spared—one hundred, twenty thousand people repented and Jonah asks God to take his life. What a contrast to Jeremiah, the prophet who wept over God's people.

MICAH

Outline of Micah

Ch 1–3	Imminent Judgment
Ch 4–5	Promise of Restoration
Ch 6	God Pleads with His People
Ch 7	Micah Resolves to Wait for Mercy

Summary of Micah

Micah preached to both Jerusalem and Samaria. He denounces their sins of idolatry, violence, oppression, robbery, divination, bribery and even prophesying for money. In the midst of these sins is a ray of hope, a future ruler coming out of Bethlehem, one who will subdue their iniquities and cast all their sins into the depths of the sea (5:2, 7:19).

NAHUM

Outline of Nahum

Ch 1—3   Woe to Nineveh

Summary of Nahum

The revival in Nineveh, started by Jonah's message one hundred fifty years ago, has fizzled out, and now Nahum brings the final message of judgment against her. Nineveh, the mightiest city on earth, with walls surrounding the city one hundred fifty feet high and sixty miles around, and with 1200 towers rising up an additional one hundred feet feet high, seemed invincible. Destruction did come as predicted in 1:8 by flood and 3:15 by fire. Nineveh is no more.

HABAKKUK

Outline of Habakkuk

Ch 1–3   From Trouble to Trust

Summary of Habakkuk

Habakkuk, seeing the wickedness of his own people, questions God on how long will this go on. God answers that He'll raise up the Chaldeans to execute judgment upon His people. Habakkuk then asks if the Chaldeans (who were worse than Judah) will be allowed to slay nations unopposed, but God replied they too shall be spoiled. Then Habakkuk sees a vision of the glorious Lord and reaffirms his trust in God.

ZEPHANIAH

Outline of Zephaniah

Ch 1–3   Judgment and Restoration

Summary of Zephaniah

Zephaniah boldly preaches of the "Day of the Lord," God's judgment which is to come upon the whole earth, in graphic detail. He speaks of judgment against Judah and surrounding nations, including Nineveh (2:13). A remnant shall remain, though, who will follow God and receive His love, His joy, and restoration.

HAGGAI

Outline of Haggai

Ch 1	Wrong Priorities—Blessings Dry Up
Ch 2	Right Priorities—Blessings Return

Summary of Haggai

Haggai preaches to the Jews who have returned to Jerusalem after the seventy-year captivity in Babylon. The people have become preoccupied with building their own homes, and God's Temple lay desolate for years. (Ezra 4-6 gives background on the hindrances to building the Temple.)

Haggai's and Zechariah's prophesying encourages the people and they continue to build. God promises the glory of the latter house shall be greater than the former (under Solomon), and God Himself will overthrow thrones and heathen kingdoms to bless His people.

ZECHARIAH

Outline of Zechariah

Ch 1—6	Ten Visions of Zechariah
Ch 7—8	Four Messages of Zechariah
Ch 9—11	Rejection of the Messiah
Ch 12—14	Reign of the Messiah

Summary of Zechariah

God used Zechariah, a younger contemporary of Haggai, to encourage His people to continue to rebuild the Temple in Jerusalem after the Jews returned from the Babylonian captivity. Zechariah saw many visions, and writes many prophecies about the coming Messiah.

MALACHI

Outline of Malachi

Summary of Malachi

About a hundred years after the Jews returned to Jerusalem, released from Babylonian captivity, God's people had become slack in their religious and moral service to God. The priests offered polluted bread, improper animal sacrifices, and held God's practices in contempt. Judah married pagan wives, were corrupt in business dealings, practiced sorcery and adultery, and robbed God of tithes and offerings.

Malachi admonished them to return to God so God's blessings can return to them. God will surely punish the wicked, so repent and deal treacherously no more.

MATTHEW

Outline of Matthew

Ch 1–2	Jesus' Genealogy and Birth
Ch 3 – 4	Jesus' Preparation for Ministry
Ch 5–7	Sermon on the Mount
Ch 8–10	Miracles and Apostles
Ch 11–16	Opposition and the Kingdom
Ch 17–25	Teaching the People
Ch 26–28	Jesus' Final Days
	Death and Resurrection

Summary of Matthew

Matthew starts his account of the life of Jesus Christ with a genealogy that shows that he is the seed of David, from the line of the kings of Judah. This gospel was written to the Jews to show that Jesus was the promised Messiah. More quotes from the Old Testament appear here than in the other gospels.

Matthew gives a detailed account of Jesus' family's flight to Egypt from King Herod, Jesus' baptism and temptation in the wilderness. After the Sermon on the Mount, we see many miracles of Jesus, and opposition from the religious leaders.

He teaches much on the kingdom of heaven, and demonstrates the gospel with signs following. After sharing on events to come in the End Times, he is betrayed by Judas, crucified, entombed and resurrected. He commands his followers to teach all nations to observe the things he commanded them, spreading the gospel to end of the earth.

MARK

Outline of Mark

Ch 1—2	Beginning of Ministry
Ch 3—12	Ministry Among Opposition
Ch 13	End Time Events
Ch 14—16	Jesus' Last Days
	Death and Resurrection

Summary of Mark

The Gospel of Mark is a short, action—packed account of the ministry of Jesus Christ, written to a Roman audience. There is more emphasis on the works of Jesus as he served the people, than long sermons as recorded in the other Gospels.

Mark 10:43—44 summarizes the presentation of Christ in this gospel: "But whosoever will be great among you, shall be your minister: And whosoever of you will be the chiefest, shall be servant of all." It's more than fitting for Mark to end his gospel with action—signs following believers doing the works of Jesus!

LUKE

Outline of Luke

Ch 1–3	John the Baptist and Jesus
Ch 4–8	Miracles and Teachings
Ch 9–10	Apostles and Seventy Sent
Ch 11–21	Teachings
Ch 22–24	Final Days
	Death and Resurrection

Summary of Luke

Luke was perhaps the only Gentile writer of the Bible. Colossians 4:14 tells us Luke was a physician, and we know he also wrote the book of Acts. Luke's Gospel was written to the Greeks, and shows the compassion of Jesus Christ to all people, Jew and Gentile, male and female, rich and poor. Many parables included here are not found in the other gospels.

We see a more complete picture of events in Jesus' life, beginning with the prophecy of John the Baptist's birth (Jesus' cousin) and Jesus' genealogy through David's son Nathan, up to his mother Mary. Luke shares many prayers and praises not recorded elsewhere. Much detail on the ministry of Jesus shows him teaching, praying, and ministering to those in need. Luke ends with Jesus' promise to send the Holy Spirit to empower them to preach of him to all nations.

JOHN

Outline of John

Summary of John

The Gospel of John reflects a very intimate view of Jesus, different from the other gospels. We get a close-up revelation of who Jesus is, and in-depth insight on his teachings that only one who was close to him could give. Many teachings from Matthew, Mark and Luke are not in John's Gospel. The intended audience was both believers and the world at large.

John shows the deity of Jesus, the Word (which was God) made flesh. In chapter one, we see that Jesus, the Word, is the beginning of all things. He called his disciples, and began performing miracles and teaching.

The dialogue between Jesus and religious leaders reflects Jesus' knowledge of the adversary being behind their opposition. John records Jesus' lengthy teaching to his disciples before his crucifixion, and his prayer in the garden of Gethsemane.

This gospel was written "that ye might believe that Jesus is the Christ, the Son of God; and that believing ye might have life through his name" (20:31).

ACTS

Outline of Acts

Ch 1—7	Spread of Christianity in Jerusalem: Peter to the Jews
Ch 8—12	Christianity in Judea and Samaria: Philip to the Samaritans
Ch 13—28	Christianity to all the Earth: Paul to the Gentiles

Summary of Acts

Act 1:8 summarizes the events taking place in the book of Acts: "But ye shall receive power, after that the Holy Ghost is come upon you: and ye shall be witnesses unto me both in Jerusalem, and in all Judea, and in Samaria, and unto the uttermost part of the earth."

On the day of Pentecost, the Holy Spirit came upon the one hundred-twenty believers in the upper room and the Church was born. The gospel spread through the apostles and believers; Peter, Philip and Paul playing significant roles. Persecution of the Church caused Christianity to spread beyond Jerusalem.

Saul, a zealous Pharisee, became a mighty voice for God to the Gentiles. (Paul was his Gentile name.) Paul's three missionary journeys helped spread the gospel to the uttermost parts of the earth. When the Jews conspired to kill Paul, he appealed to Caesar (Paul being a Roman citizen) and was taken to Rome.

Paul wrote most of the New Testament, some books written during his missionary journeys, some written while in prison.

ROMANS

Outline of Romans

Summary of Romans

In the book of Romans, the apostle Paul gives a thorough discourse on a key truth of Christianity: the believer is made righteous by faith in Jesus Christ, not by the works of the law. Those who choose a lifestyle of ungodliness will suffer eternal wrath, but those who seek to glorify God will enjoy eternal life.

Abraham, our father of faith, obtained righteousness by believing God, and the blessings of God came upon him. He and his seed (all believers) are heirs of the world (4:13), and now by God's grace we can reign in life and enjoy the blessings of Abraham.

As new creatures we are dead to sin and now walk in the Spirit, in newness of life. We are more than conquerors, secure in the love of God. As believers, we're to be transformed by the Word of God and live according to the law of love. Though Israel has rejected Christ, God will graft them in when the fullness of the Gentiles have come into Christ.

I CORINTHIANS

Outline of I Corinthians

Ch 1	God's Superior Wisdom
Ch 2	God's Revealed Wisdom
Ch 3	Wisdom Builds God's Temple
Ch 4	Paul's Faithfulness
Ch 5—6	Flee Fornication
Ch 7	Marriage
Ch 8	Food Offered to Idols
Ch 9	Paul's Defense of His Calling
Ch 10	Resist Temptation
Ch 11:1—16	Authority in the Family
Ch 11:17—34	Observance of Communion
Ch 12	Spiritual Gifts
Ch 13	Love
Ch 14	Operation of Spiritual Gifts in the Assembly
Ch 15	The Resurrection of Christ and the Church
Ch 16	Final Words

Summary of I Corinthians

Corinth, the most important city in Greece during Paul's day, was an idolatrous and immoral city. Paul gives some very specific words of correction and instruction in this letter, on a very practical level of church meetings and daily life. There were contentions, strife, envying, cliques, sexual immorality, taking the saints to secular court, eating food offered to idols, and disorder during church services.

Paul also gives lengthy instruction on observing the Lord's supper, operating in spiritual gifts, walking in love, married life, and the resurrection of Christ and of the Church.

II CORINTHIANS

Outline of II Corinthians

Ch 1	Comfort in Tribulation
Ch 2	Paul's Words of Correction
Ch 3	The Glorious Gospel
Ch 4	The Gospel Brings Strength to Endure
Ch 5	Eternal Rewards Bring Strength to Endure
Ch 6	The Grace of God to Endure
Ch 7	God's Comfort to Endure
Ch 8—9	The Grace of Giving
Ch 10—13	Paul's Suffering for the Sake of the Gospel

Summary of II Corinthians

In his second letter to the Corinthian church, Paul addresses the emergence of "false apostles" (11:13) who oppose Paul and bring in false teachings. Paul defends his call to be an apostle, and sites this church as evidence of the fruit of his work in the ministry.

Though Paul has suffered much for the sake of the gospel (he was beaten three times, stoned, imprisoned, shipwrecked, in constant danger, and suffering physical hardship, 11:23-28), he is comforted, and even joyful, in the midst of tribulation. He was caught up into Paradise and experienced things words cannot express.

Chapter 12:15 summarizes his experiences with the church at Corinth: "And I will very gladly spend and be spent for you; though the more abundantly I love you, the less I be loved."

GALATIANS

Outline of Galatians

Ch 1	Paul's Calling: From Judaism to Christ
Ch 2	Paul's Defense: Christianity Above Judaism
Ch 3	The Covenant Preceded the Law
	Faith Makes the Law Unnecessary
Ch 4	From Tutored Child to Heir
Ch 5	Flesh Life vs. Spirit Life
Ch 6	Sowing to Flesh vs. Sowing to Spirit

Summary of Galatians

As in II Corinthians, Galatians reveals personal details of Paul's calling and ministry work. He stresses repeatedly that faith in Christ activates God's covenant blessings, and we no longer need to adhere to Jewish law.

Judaizers (Jews seeking to bring believers into a legalistic, Jewish, law-based gospel) had come to Galatia after Paul left. Paul now had to undo erroneous teachings and clarifies what place the law had in the past, but is no longer necessary. The law of Love is our law, and the Holy Spirit directing our walk keeps us from walking in the flesh. If we keep sowing to the Spirit, we'll enjoy the life God originally intended for us to live.

EPHESIANS

Outline of Ephesians

Ch 1	The Church: God's Plan for Mankind
Ch 2	The Church: From Children of Wrath To Children of God
Ch 3	The Church: Gentiles Came into Christ Christ Came into the Gentiles
Ch 4	The Church: Being Perfected in Christ To Walk as Christ
Ch 5	The Church: Walking as Christ, Our Example
Ch 6	The Church: Strong in Christ Against Spiritual Attacks

Summary of Ephesians

Paul shares a vivid picture in this epistle of God's plan for the New Testament church. God planned for Jew and Gentile to be one in Christ as His family, before the foundation of the world. Even though men were disobedient, without God, and dead in sins, Christ died for all, to give us all access to God the Father, by His Spirit.

Once we're in Christ, we must grow up and mature in Him, being filled with His Spirit and taught by the gifts God placed in the body: apostles, prophets, evangelists, pastors and teachers.

The truth should work its way out into our external behavior. Daily we choose to put off the old man (of the flesh) and put on the new man (Christ) who is created in God's image and therefore walks, talks, acts, and lives like God.

Now that we're no longer influenced by darkness, we can be strong in God's strength and stand against the tricks and schemes of the devil through prayer.

PHILIPPIANS

Outline of Philippians

Ch 1   A Living Sacrifice: Paul
Ch 2   A Living Sacrifice: Christ, Our Pattern
Ch 3   A Living Sacrifice: The Mindset
Ch 4   A Living Sacrifice: The Philippian Church

Summary of Philippians

Paul's complete dedication to God and to fulfilling his life's calling is evident in his letter to the Philippian church. He lived and suffered that others would know Christ and grow in Christ.

Using Christ as his example, Paul laid aside every natural benefit of status, culture, education and heritage. All he wants is Christ, all he knows is Christ. He challenges the church to follow his example and Christ's example, and rejoices that the Philippians' care for him has flourished once again.

COLOSSIANS

Outline of Colossians

Ch 1   Filled with Christ: Redeemed from the Enemy
Ch 2   Rooted in Christ: Separated from the World
Ch 3   Putting on Christ: Mortifying the Flesh
Ch 4   Brethren in Christ: Greetings

Summary of Colossians

Jesus Christ is the central focus of Paul's letter to the church at Colossae. Very similar to the book of Ephesians, it points us to Christ, the Head of the Church, having preeminence over all things.

With every issue he addresses, Paul draws our attention back to Christ, what He accomplished for us, who He is to us, and what our lifestyle should be in Him.

I THESSALONIANS

Outline of I Thessalonians

Ch 1   The Thessalonian Church: Paul's Gospel Birthed Them

Ch 2   The Thessalonian Church: Paul's Affection for Them

Ch 3   The Thessalonian Church: Paul Establishing Them

Ch 4   The Thessalonian Church: Paul Instructing Them

Summary of I Thessalonians

It appears that the apostle Paul has a special endearment towards the church of Thessalonica. He shares openly his affection and desire towards them. He expresses his sincerity in bringing them the gospel, and encourages their faith in suffering. He assures them they haven't missed the rapture, and that wrath will come to their persecutors. Final brief words exhort them on a variety of topics regarding their conduct.

II THESSALONIANS

Outline of II Thessalonians

Ch 1	Persecution: Paul Encourages Their Faith
Ch 2	Persecutors: They Will Be Recompensed in the End Times
Ch 3	People: Exhortation to Live Orderly

Summary of II Thessalonians

Paul assures the church at Thessalonica that the suffering they were experiencing was not the tribulation. He expounds on the second coming of Christ, and reveals facts concerning the coming of the anti-christ. He ends with addressing issues of saints walking disorderly among them.

I TIMOTHY

Outline of I Timothy

Ch 1	Quench Wrong Doctrines:
	The Law is not for the Righteous
Ch 2	Have the Church to Pray
	Keep the Women Under Authority
Ch 3	Select Qualified Leadership
Ch 4	Avoid False Doctrines
	Be an Example
Ch 5	Relating to the Flock
	Caring for Widows
	Correcting Elders
Ch 6	Servants and Masters
	Pursuing Godliness
	The Fight of Faith
	Instructions to the Rich

Summary of I Timothy

Paul had assigned Timothy to pastor the church in Ephesus, but challenges regarding Timothy's youthful age were discouraging him. Timothy, along with Silas and Luke, accompanied Paul extensively in traveling to establish churches. Paul considered Timothy his "son in the faith" and shared many insights to assist Timothy in his leadership of the flock.

Paul covered many areas relating to the church: maintaining correct doctrine, prayer, women submitting to authority, qualifications for bishops and deacons (and their wives); using the gift given him in ministry; how to relate to the men, women and widows; servants, the rich, and Timothy's personal faith walk.

II TIMOTHY

Outline of II Timothy

Ch 1   Exhortation: Use Your Spiritual Resources
Ch 2   Endure and Take Charge
Ch 3   In Perilous Times, Stay with the Word
Ch 4   Preach the Word and Endure Afflictions
        Paul, Timothy's Example

Summary of II Timothy

Paul's second letter to Timothy was written during his second imprisonment—very different from the first one in Rome, where he was under house arrest. The Roman emperor Nero (A.D. 54-68) blamed the Christians for the fire that destroyed half of Rome in A.D. 64, and began great persecution and torture of Christians. It was now illegal to practice Christianity in the Roman empire, so Paul's persecutors were now backed by civil law. It is thought that Paul was arrested suddenly, and had to leave his coat, books and scripture scrolls (4:13). Believers feared for their own lives and abandoned Paul.

Though in a cold, Roman cell, accused as an evil doer (2:9), Paul encourages Timothy to preach the Word, endure perilous times, and raise up others to teach the Word. Paul knows he is soon to depart this earth, and leaves a final word regarding his earthly ministry:

"For I am now ready to be offered, and the time of my departure is at hand.

I have fought a good fight, I have finished my course, I have kept the faith:

Henceforth there is laid up for me a crown of righteousness, which the Lord, the righteous judge, shall give me at that day: and not to me only, but unto all them also that love his appearing" (II Timothy 4:6-8).

TITUS

Outline of Titus

Ch 1	Charge: Bring Order and Correction
	Appoint Church Leadership
	Character Qualities of a Bishop
Ch 2	Teach the Men, Women, Servants
Ch 3	Teach Obedience to Authority
	Maintain Good Works

Summary of Titus

Titus was another of Paul's "sons in the faith" (1:4), a Gentile, assigned to bring order and leadership to the church that had already been started on the island of Crete.

The Cretans had a reputation for being "liars, evil brutes, and lazy gluttons" (NIV). There were those who professed to know God, but whose actions and teachings were deceptive and reprobate (morally depraved and unprincipled), whose mouths must be stopped.

Paul told Titus to appoint elders in every city, and gave qualifications for service. He shared specific instructions on what to teach the men, and how the older women should teach the younger women. Paul wrote that Titus himself should be an example, and shouldn't talk about how bad they are (for we were all disobedient at one time), but admonish them to maintain good works.

PHILEMON

Outline of Philemon

Ch 1   Paul's Appeal to Philemon to Forgive
        and Restore Onesimus

Summary of Philemon

Onesimus, a former slave to Philemon, had run away, and gotten saved under Paul's ministry. Now Paul writes Philemon, asking him not only to forgive Onesimus, but to receive him back as a brother, who can be of better service to him as a believer. Paul pledges to repay any financial hardship that Onesimus has caused, in spite of the fact that Philemon owes Paul his very life.

HEBREWS

Outline of Hebrews

Ch 1   The Son, Superior to Prophets
The Son, Superior to Angels
Ch 2   The Son, Superior over the Devil
Ch 3   The Son, Superior to Moses
Christ's House, Superior to Moses' House
Ch 4   God's Rest, Superior to Israel's Rest
Ch 5   The Son, Superior High Priest
Ch 6   Believer's Call to a Higher Faith
Ch 7   Jesus, A Superior High Priest
A Superior Priesthood
Ch 8   New Covenant, Superior to the Old
Ch 9   Christ the Lamb, A Superior Sacrifice
Ch 10   The Church, Sanctified and Perfected
Ch 11   God's Hall of the Diligent in Faith
Ch 12   Appropriating Grace to Endure
Ch 13   Final Instructions

Summary of Hebrews

The book of Hebrews was written to Jewish believers to prevent them from falling back into Judaism to escape persecution. The writer presents the work of Christ as being in every way superior to what the law had to offer. Christ, in His death as the perfect sacrifice, and His present ministry as High Priest of good things to come, made the Jewish priesthood and practices obsolete. He was the ultimate fulfillment of the types and shadows of the Old Testament.

The saints in chapter 11 walked by faith. God honored the faith of those who lived before the law and those who lived under the law. Jesus, the author and perfecter of our faith, was able to endure the cross, so we believers can endure also, as we walk by faith and keep the promises of God in view.

JAMES

Outline of James

Summary of James

James, the half-brother of Jesus, full brother of Jude (writer of the epistle Jude), first pastor of the Jerusalem church, wrote this epistle to the Jews living away from Jerusalem.

James insisted that believers' works must accompany their faith, or their faith is dead. By faith we must access wisdom, endure trials, bridle our tongues, treat all men fairly, and pray. This is a very practical book with simple truths that all believers can apply to their lives.

I PETER

Outline of I Peter

Ch 1	Conforming to Christ During Trials
Ch 2	Feed on the Word, Walk in the Word
Ch 3	Living the Word, A Witness to the Unbeliever
Ch 4	Suffer as a Christian, Glorify God
Ch 5	Exhortation to Elders

Summary of I Peter

Peter writes words of encouragement to believers who are suffering for their faith, using Christ as an example to follow (2:21). Peter makes a distinction between suffering for faults and ungodly behavior, and suffering as a Christian. As Christ was rejected, so are believers, but we must continue to love one another and not get pulled into the flesh.

Husbands and wives, servants and masters, citizens and civil authorities, elders and sheep, brother and brother—Peter instructs them to let every relationship reflect a Christ-like attitude and conduct. Peter always points them back to God's Word, which will help them grow and mature. Lastly, he warns them to be vigilant not to let the adversary devour them. After they have suffered a while, God will perfect them, establish them, strengthen them, and settle them.

II PETER

Outline of II Peter

Summary of II Peter

Peter lifts up a high standard in chapter one, saying that through the knowledge of God and His promises we partake of His divine nature, and will not partake of the corruption spawned by the flesh. He emphasizes Christian attributes such as virtue, temperance, patience, godliness and charity.

In Peter's first letter, opposition to the Church was coming from without. In II Peter, attacks are coming from within: from false prophets and teachers, bringing heresies and ungodly living; and from people walking in the flesh, in sin. Peter assures them that the unjust will surely be punished in the day of judgment.

Lastly, though scoffers mock them because Christ has not come back yet, Peter admonishes them to stay holy, godly, and without blame, because the Day of the Lord will surely come.

I JOHN

Outline of I John

Ch 1	Fellowship with God's Family
Ch 2	Walking in the Word is Walking in Love
	The Holy Spirit Will Keep You in the Truth and Away from the World
Ch 3	The Influence of Sin vs. The Influence of the New Birth
Ch 4	Spirit of Anti-Christ vs. Spirit of God
	God Loved Us, We Love One Another
Ch 5	Our Faith Overcomes the World
	We Have Eternal Life
	We Have Answered Prayer
	We Have Immunity From the Wicked One

Summary of I John

The apostle John's sweet fellowship with the Lord Jesus during His life continued after His resurrection, and in this epistle to John's "children" in the faith, he seeks to enlighten the reader to join him in this glorious fellowship.

Requirements for enjoying this fellowship include: walking in the light; confessing our sins and receiving forgiveness and cleansing; walking in love toward our brother; not loving the world but overcoming it; being taught by the Holy Spirit; staying free from sin; avoiding false prophets; loving God; partaking of eternal life; asking and receiving from God; and knowing God. John spends a great deal of time illustrating how a believer should walk in love.

II JOHN

Outline of II John

Ch 1   Love is Walking in God's Commandments
        Don't Fellowship with an Anti-Christ

Summary of II John

John writes to "the elect lady" and her children. He compliments the children for walking in truth and admonishes the lady to walk in love, which is walking in God's commandments. He then says not to entertain deceivers that don't abide in the doctrine of Christ, so she'll not lose what she's gained thus far. He ends with a greeting from the children of her elect sister.

Theologians state he may be addressing an actual "lady" or a church body of believers.

III JOHN

Outline of III John

Ch 1   Gaius' Walk in Truth and Charity
              Diotrephes' Evil Works
              Demetrius' Good Report

Summary of III John

John compliments his brother in Christ, Gaius, who shows hospitality and charity to both missionaries and strangers.

John then shares that Diotrephes, (perhaps the church elder), refused John's letter, and maliciously maligned John, and threatened to cast men out of the church for receiving him.

In contrast, Demetrius (perhaps another church leader) has a good report, before men and the truth. Gaius is admonished not to follow that which is evil, for those who do evil have not seen God, but to follow those who do good and are of God.

JUDE

Outline of Jude

Ch 1   Ungodly Teachings-Contend for the Faith
Ungodly Men-Warning Against Them
Ungodly Men-God's Judgment Upon Them
Ungodly Times-Believer's Steadfastness in
Them

Summary of Jude

The entire book of Jude shows the picture of an apostate church of the End Times—a church that has abandoned it's faith as a result of receiving erroneous teachings of ungodly men.

Though many New Testament epistles address the threat of false teachers rising up in the church, Jude passionately expounds upon their ultimate punishment and even quotes Enoch's prophecy (not found in our Old Testament scriptures) of the Lord's second coming with His saints to execute judgment upon the ungodly.

Jude's advice to the saints living in an era of such ungodliness is to keep themselves in the love of God, have compassion, make a difference, save those falling into "the fire" and to build themselves up in the faith, praying in the Holy Ghost.

REVELATION

Outline of Revelation

Ch 1:1 – 8	The Revelation of Jesus Christ
Ch 1:9 – 20	Jesus Christ's Assignment to John
Ch 2 – 3	Letters to the Seven Churches in Asia
Ch 4 – 5	Events in Heaven's Throne Room
Ch 6– 8:5	The Seven Seals of Judgment
Ch 8:6–11	The Seven Trumpets of Judgment
Ch 12–14	Prophetic Scenes in Heaven and Earth
Ch 15–16	The Seven Vials of Judgment
Ch 17–18	The Final Destruction of Babylon
Ch 19	The Second Coming of Christ
Ch 20	Millennium Events
Ch 21	Prophetic Scenes from the New Heaven and the New Earth
Ch 22	Jesus' Final Words

Summary of Revelation

The book of Revelation records the visions of John as Jesus Christ revealed to him events surrounding the future of the Church, Israel, satan and his followers, and the end of the world and its ungodly systems.

The apostle John, while exiled as a prisoner on the island of Patmos, was caught up in the Spirit, and shown tremendous end-time events. First, he was instructed to write letters to seven churches to warn them to stop compromising and return to being the "Overcomers" God intended them to be. (Only the Overcomers would go in the rapture, and the marginal, compromising "believers" would be left on earth, and given the opportunity to repent and get right during the first half of the tribulation.) (Ch 2-3)

Next we see a praise service in the Throne Room of God

in heaven, after the Overcomers have been raptured. Jesus has a sealed book, and as He opens each of the seven seals, tragic events take place on earth and in the heavens surrounding the earth. At the end of the first half of the tribulation is another rapture of believers, repentant and saved during this time. One hundred forty-four thousand Jewish believers on earth are sealed for protection from the tragic events still to come. (Ch 4-7)

When the angels blow the seven trumpets, massive fire attacks hit and devastate the earth. Millions of demons attack the survivors, and no one repents. Two witnesses (many believe they are Moses and Elijah) are sent by God to earth, with great power to call down fire, stop the rain, turn water to blood and command plagues onto the earth. They are killed, and the world rejoices; but they resurrect in three and a half days and ascend to heaven. (Ch 8-11)

The anti-christ arises as head of the beast (a federation of nations controlled by satan, the dragon, seeking to rule the earth). The false prophet seduces men to worship an image of the beast and take his number 666. (Many believe 666 represents the "unholy trinity" consisting of the devil, the anti—christ and the false prophet.) John sees many other visions, including another group of one hundred forty-four thousand (this time they are in heaven), and then the seven golden vials of judgment are poured out. They are full of the wrath of God, and His full vengeance is poured out upon the earth. At the end of the seven-year tribulation period, satan gathers the nations of the earth to come against Israel in the battle of Armageddon. Jesus comes back to earth with His saints and they wipe out the whole army. Babylon (religious, political and economic Babylon) falls in ultimate defeat and destruction. The beast and the false prophet are cast alive into the lake of fire. (Ch 12-19)

Now the millennium is at hand. Satan is bound for one thousand years in the bottomless pit. Those who were beheaded for the witness of Jesus and the Word of God will reign with Christ a thousand years on the earth. (This is the first resurrection.) At the end of the thousand years, satan is loosed from prison to deceive the nations one last time, and convince them to join him in battle. Fire from God out of heaven devours them. The devil is cast into the lake of fire and brimstone. The unrighteous dead are brought before the Great White Throne Judgment, and judged according to their works. They all, along with death and hell, are cast into the lake of fire. (Ch 20)

We now see a panorama of a new heaven and a new earth; and the bride, the Lamb's wife, coming down from heaven, the New Jerusalem. What a beautiful city, made of gold, pearls and precious stones, lit by the glory of God! The nations still alive bring their glory and honor to it. No more curse. Christ and His Church shall reign forever and ever. Jesus rewards his people with their work assignments in His eternal kingdom. Jesus said He comes quickly.

Let us learn from these prophecies revealed to the apostle John, and stay stirred up and on fire for God, serving Him all the days of our lives! (Ch 21-22)

To order more copies of this book
Phone: 800-711-9327
or visit www.billwinston.org

Bible Reading Instructions

Welcome to the world of the revelation knowledge of God! Reading through God's Word provides a foundation of wisdom that never becomes outdated, and lasts for eternity. Here are a few suggestions to get you started.

1. If you enjoy a consistent Bible reading routine of three and a quarter chapters a day for 365 days in the year, then make your plan and cross off the chapters as you read. Beware that some chapters are extremely long, so those three chapters may take longer on some days.

2. You may want to designate a certain number of minutes to read daily. Just record which chapter and verse you stopped at when the timer dings!

3. Perhaps week days you prefer to read fewer chapters daily, and weekends read more.

4. You may want to read some books in their entirety, in one sitting. That's the best way to get an overall scope of the book.

5. Some like reading in the morning, some in the evening, some during the lunch hour.

6. You may want to set a goal for the number of chapters to read in a given week or month. You can start in Genesis, skip around, or read from the Old and New Testament daily. This is a good way to ease into reading the Bible through in a year.

Whatever your preferred method, the important thing is to just get started! God really does speak to us through our Bible reading time, and it may provoke some in-depth study as He pulls back the curtain and shows you secrets and mysteries of His Kingdom.

For variety, you can alternate Bible translations if it gets challenging to remain faithful. There are a few chapters, I must admit, that are less interesting, with repetitive lists. Don't feel shy about quickly perusing through those segments. Before you know it, you'll be using biblical examples in your everyday conversation!

This recording chart is also available as a free download. Please visit www.livingwd.org to download the file and print.

Mark a "/" or an "X" in each box after you have completed reading the corresponding chapter.

The Law or Books of Moses - 5										
Genesis	1	2	3	4	5	6	7	8	9	10
	11	12	13	14	15	16	17	18	19	20
	21	22	23	24	25	26	27	28	29	30
	31	32	33	34	35	36	37	38	39	40
	41	42	43	44	45	46	47	48	49	50
Exodus	1	2	3	4	5	6	7	8	9	10
	11	12	13	14	15	16	17	18	19	20
	21	22	23	24	25	26	27	28	29	30
	31	32	33	34	35	36	37	38	39	40
Leviticus	1	2	3	4	5	6	7	8	9	10
	11	12	13	14	15	16	17	18	19	20
	21	22	23	24	25	26	27			
Numbers	1	2	3	4	5	6	7	8	9	10
	11	12	13	14	15	16	17	18	19	20
	21	22	23	24	25	26	27	28	29	30
	31	32	33	34	35	36				
Deuteronomy	1	2	3	4	5	6	7	8	9	10
	11	12	13	14	15	16	17	18	19	20
	21	22	23	24	25	26	27	28	29	30
	31	32	33	34						
The Books of History - 12										
Joshua	1	2	3	4	5	6	7	8	9	10
	11	12	13	14	15	16	17	18	19	20
	21	22	23	24						
Judges	1	2	3	4	5	6	7	8	9	10
	11	12	13	14	15	16	17	18	19	20
	21									
Ruth	1	2	3	4						

1 Samuel	1	2	3	4	5	6	7	8	9	10
	11	12	13	14	15	16	17	18	19	20
	21	22	23	24	25	26	27	28	29	30
	31									
2 Samuel	1	2	3	4	5	6	7	8	9	10
	11	12	13	14	15	16	17	18	19	20
	21	22	23	24						
1 Kings	1	2	3	4	5	6	7	8	9	10
	11	12	13	14	15	16	17	18	19	20
	21	22								
2 Kings	1	2	3	4	5	6	7	8	9	10
	11	12	13	14	15	16	17	18	19	20
	21	22	23	24	25					
1 Chronicles	1	2	3	4	5	6	7	8	9	10
	11	12	13	14	15	16	17	18	19	20
	21	22	23	24	25	26	27	28	29	
2 Chronicles	1	2	3	4	5	6	7	8	9	10
	11	12	13	14	15	16	17	18	19	20
	21	22	23	24	25	26	27	28	29	30
	31	32	33	34	35	36				
Ezra	1	2	3	4	5	6	7	8	9	10
Nehemiah	1	2	3	4	5	6	7	8	9	10
Esther	1	2	3	4	5	6	7	8	9	10
The Books of Poetry - 5										
Job	1	2	3	4	5	6	7	8	9	10
	11	12	13	14	15	16	17	18	19	20
	21	22	23	24	25	26	27	28	29	30
	31	32	33	34	35	36	37	38	39	40
	41	42								
Psalms	1	2	3	4	5	6	7	8	9	10
	11	12	13	14	15	16	17	18	19	20
	21	22	23	24	25	26	27	28	29	30
	31	32	33	34	35	36	37	38	39	40
	41	42	43	44	45	46	47	48	49	50
	51	52	53	54	55	56	57	58	59	60

Psalms	61	62	63	64	65	66	67	68	69	
	71	72	73	74	75	76	77	78	79	80
	81	82	83	84	85	86	87	88	89	90
	91	92	93	94	95	96	97	98	99	100
	101	102	103	104	105	106	107	108	109	110
	111	112	113	114	115	116	117	118	119	120
	121	122	123	124	125	126	127	128	129	130
	131	132	133	134	135	136	137	138	139	140
	141	142	143	144	145	146	147	148	149	150
Proverbs	1	2	3	4	5	6	7	8	9	10
	11	12	13	14	15	16	17	18	19	20
	21	22	23	24	25	26	27	28	29	30
	31									
Ecclesiastes	1	2	3	4	5	6	7	8	9	10
	11	12								
Song of Solomon	1	2	3	4	5	6	7	8		
The Major Books of Prophecy - 5										
Isaiah	1	2	3	4	5	6	7	8	9	10
	11	12	13	14	15	16	17	18	19	20
	21	22	23	24	25	26	27	28	29	30
	31	32	33	34	35	36	37	38	39	40
	41	42	43	44	45	46	47	48	49	50
	51	52	53	54	55	56	57	58	59	60
	61	62	63	64	65	66				
Jeremiah	1	2	3	4	5	6	7	8	9	10
	11	12	13	14	15	16	17	18	19	20
	21	22	23	24	25	26	27	28	29	30
	31	32	33	34	35	36	37	38	39	40
	41	42	43	44	45	46	47	48	49	50
	51	52								
Lamentations	1	2	3	4	5					
Ezekiel	1	2	3	4	5	6	7	8	9	10
	11	12	13	14	15	16	17	18	19	20
	21	22	23	24	25	26	27	28	29	30

Ezekiel	31	32	33	34	35	36	37	38	39	40
	41	42	43	44	45	46	47	48		
Daniel	1	2	3	4	5	6	7	8	9	10
	11	12								

The Minor Books of Prophecy - 12

Hosea	1	2	3	4	5	6	7	8	9	10
	11	12	13	14						
Joel	1	2	3							
Amos	1	2	3	4	5	6	7	8	9	
Obadiah	1									
Jonah	1	2	3	4						
Micah	1	2	3	4	5	6	7			
Nahum	1	2	3							
Habakkuk	1	2	3							
Zephaniah	1	2	3							
Haggai	1	2								
Zechariah	1	2	3	4	5	6	7	8	9	10
Malachi	1	2	3	4						

The Gospels - 4

Matthew	1	2	3	4	5	6	7	8	9	10
	11	12	13	14	15	16	17	18	19	20
	21	22	23	24	25	26	27	28		
Mark	1	2	3	4	5	6	7	8	9	10
	11	12	13	14	15	16				
Luke	1	2	3	4	5	6	7	8	9	10
	11	12	13	14	15	16	17	18	19	20
	21	22	23	24						
John	1	2	3	4	5	6	7	8	9	10
	11	12	13	14	15	16	17	18	19	20
	21									

History of The Early Church - 1

Acts	1	2	3	4	5	6	7	8	9	10
	11	12	13	14	15	16	17	18	19	20
	21	22	23	24	25	26	27	28		

Letters of Paul - 13										
Romans	1	2	3	4	5	6	7	8	9	10
	11	12	13	14	15	16				
I Corinthians	1	2	3	4	5	6	7	8	9	10
	11	12	13	14	15	16				
2 Corinthians	1	2	3	4	5	6	7	8	9	10
	11	12	13							
Galatians	1	2	3	4	5	6				
Ephesians	1	2	3	4	5	6				
Philippians	1	2	3	4						
Colossians	1	2	3	4						
I Thessalonians	1	2	3	4	5					
2 Thessalonians	1	2	3							
1 Timothy	1	2	3	4	5	6				
2 Timothy	1	2	3	4						
Titus	1	2	3							
Philemon	1									
General Letters - 8										
Hebrews	1	2	3	4	5	6	7	8	9	10
	11	12	13							
James	1	2	3	4	5					
1 Peter	1	2	3	4	5					
2 Peter	1	2	3							
1 John	1	2	3	4	5					
2 John	1									
3 John	1									
Jude	1									
Book of Prophecy - 1										
Revelation	1	2	3	4	5	6	7	8	9	10
	11	12	13	14	15	16	17	18	19	20
	21	22								